How to Create a Business

The Best Way to Plan and Develop Your Big Idea

Table of Contents

Introduction 1

Chapter 1: Your Big Idea 3

Chapter 2: Developing Your Idea 18

Chapter 3: Building Your Plans 30

Chapter 4: A Blueprint for Success 43

Chapter 5: Don't Forget These Important Tips! 53

Conclusion 61

Introduction

Thank you and congratulations for purchasing *"How to Create a Business:* The Best Way to Plan and Develop Your Big Idea"!

This book was designed to help you take a business idea and develop it to the point that you can generate and implement a powerful plan that will take your idea and turn it into a reality.

Through a series of steps and practices, you will be given the exact blueprint needed to create a business so strong that it withstands the trials and tribulations that many new businesses face. As a result, you will be able to rely on your business to carry you forward, enjoying the greatest success possible.

Whether you already have an idea or not, this book will help you get started. You will learn in Chapter 1 all that is required for you to choose a strong idea, and how you can get extremely clear on what it is. It may seem inconceivable now, but soon you will be able to discuss your business idea with such clarity that it will seem inevitable for it to eventually come into reality! Once you have, you will learn how to develop your idea, build a plan, and how you can implement that plan to generate maximum success. Finally, you will be walked through some incredible tips that will promote a strong and successful business plan.

By the end of this book, you will have a plan that you can use to completely develop your busines. If you are ready to stop dreaming about the business world and start bringing those dreams into reality, read on! And of course, enjoy!

Chapter 1: Your Big Idea

Hey! What's the big idea? No really, what? When you are starting a business, any business, it always starts with an idea. This is a theory or a dream that you have for a business. You use this dream as the seed for everything else to grow from. Whether you have one or not, we will explore the realm of business ideas, and how you can ensure that you have a clear idea that you can later develop a plan from.

If you already have a business idea, you may find that some of the practices in this chapter are not as beneficial to you as others. However, I still recommend that you complete them. In the early stages, ideas tend to shift and transform over time. By completing the practices laid out in this book, you can ensure that the idea you have chosen will fit well with you and that you have considered all aspects of it.

If you have not already come up with an idea, fear not! The following steps will help you decide what you might consider for your business idea. Each step will help you identify which ideas will be the most successful in the long run, so ensure that you take your time and consider each one carefully.

Remember, the idea is the entire foundation for everything. This is the seed from which the rest of your business will grow. If you want to have a powerful business, you need to start with a powerful and effective plan. We will ensure that you have a plan so strong that everything else will fall into place easily. If your plan is too weak, not clarified, or otherwise features pitfalls, there is a good chance that it will not work out for a true business model. Some businesses are better to remain as ideas, rather than actual businesses. For that reason, it is crucial that you are very critical of each step and that you think about everything. Just to be safe, even if you already have an idea, you may want to consider alternatives as you work through these steps. This doesn't necessarily mean you have to wander away from your original idea, but it will help you determine if there is a different area or angle that may be better for your business to be built on.

Step One: Look for Opportunity

The first step in finding a business idea is looking for areas of opportunity. While not every opportunity will be one worth taking, the more opportunities you look for, the more likely you are to find the one that you should follow through on.

Opportunities are fairly broad when it comes to this step. You want to essentially teach yourself to see where opportunities lie and discover exactly what the said opportunity is. For example, perhaps you are in a changing room, and you realize that it would be helpful if they had a spot where you could hang your phone and take timed pictures of yourself so that you would remember which clothes looked good on you and which didn't. While this isn't necessarily a "good" opportunity, it is certainly an opportunity. Learning to see all of the opportunities you come across is a good way to open your mind and keep yourself available for when the perfect opportunity comes your way.

As you come across opportunities, consider writing them down. Then, later on, you can revisit each opportunity you noticed and see if any of them are actually good or not. Some people have "ah-ha" moments that they use to determine whether or not an idea is good or not. For example, they may come across many opportunities, but a single one seems to really stand out, and they consider it to be a great opportunity. This would likely spark them into action and get them started on creating an idea, and maybe even a plan. For others, particularly those who are cautious or not yet experienced, it may not be this easy for you to find your perfect idea. Instead, if you had them written down, you could later research them and consider if any would actually be feasible or not.

Looking for opportunity is something that you should never stop doing, even once you have a business idea in place. While you aren't likely to pursue two or three ideas at once, taking the best one and running with it is a great way to start. Then, if you find that you have time to start on a new idea later, you will already have a few ideas on the back burner.

Step Two: Find Problems

After you have come across some potential opportunities, you need to start learning to look for problems. Every single business that exists solves some form of problem for their clients. Computer technicians fix broken computers, fashion stores provide solutions for individuals to clothe themselves in their own unique style, even universities are built based on providing educational solutions. Every business you look into is using the word "solution" in some way, ultimately meaning that they exist to solve a problem.

If you want a strong business idea, you need one that is rooted in a problem that many people face. So, consider the opportunity and start looking for all of the potential problems that people would face as a result of the opportunity you are considering. For example, your page may look something like this:

- **Opportunity:** Holders for cell phones so you can take images of your potential outfits in the change room, helping you recall how well they worked later on.

- **Problem:** Arms are too short, so you cannot get a picture of your entire outfit without chopping some

7

part of you out. As well, the strange distorted angle you take it on will change how the outfit looks on you.

- **Problem:** You like something on the rack, try it on, and by the time you get to check out you have forgotten which item had the neckline you didn't like as much. You end up buying said item, and it isn't until you get home later that you realize you weren't a big fan of the item once it was on.

- **Problem:** Dressing in change rooms and running out into the hallway to show the outfit off to friends can be difficult, requires you to show it off to everyone, and often clutters the hallway. Sometimes, change rooms don't even have a space for people to wait and see. Pictures on your phone would help your shopping partner determine whether or not the outfits looked good.

Do you get the point? The idea is that you want to discover as many problems as you can be surrounding the idea you have considered. Write down every possible problem you can think of, no matter how large or small it may seem. You want to exhaust all options.

Looking for problems helps you with two things: first, it tells you if a viable problem actually exists. If it does, then it justifies a solution. If it doesn't, there may not be a solution that people are actually willing to invest in. Second, looking at problems may help you discover new opportunities. For example, maybe you discover that the original idea you thought of was good, but in the process, you discover an entirely new opportunity you can use that is far better.

It is good practice to look at the potential problems for every opportunity that passes as a "good" one. So, some opportunities you will know right away that they are good in theory but would not pass well in an actual business model. Others, you may genuinely consider. For these ones, look at all potential problems. Even if you discover that there isn't a big enough problem to be solved, or that the problem can be solved, but you realize that you do not have the resources to do it effectively, this helps you learn how to evaluate opportunities. You begin to discover what types of problems exist and what opportunities surround them. And again, through exploring the problems, you may just find a new (and completely viable) opportunity that becomes your next big thing!

Step Three: Find Solutions

For every problem you write down in step two, find solutions. This is the part of the process where you get to see how viable the problems actually are. This will also likely be the part where you might come up with a completely new opportunity based on the solutions to the problems you have already explored.

Once again, write down any solution, no matter how ridiculous it might sound. Remember, someone somewhere has invented something far sillier than the answers you are coming up with right now. Also, no one will read this list except you.

The process of coming up with solutions is a good way for you to realize what solutions are available for what problems. It will also help you expand your ability to evaluate opportunities even further by being able to quickly think of both problems and solutions that will come from any opportunity you consider. The more you practice this on paper, the faster you will get over time. Then, who knows, you may just find yourself experiencing your own "ah-ha" moment at some point in the near future!

Step Four: Consider Your Passions

Once you have a series of opportunities, complete with viable problems and solutions, you want to narrow them down. Naturally, some of them will be knocked off simply because they were not strong enough to actually build a business on. However, many will likely remain on the list because they are actually reasonable options. For this reason, you need to consider your passions!

The reason why you need to consider your passions may be obvious, but when we follow something that we are genuinely passionate about, we are far more likely to actually experience success in it. This is because you know more about the topic, you are excited by the topic, and you are eager to work with the topic. The work you are doing is enjoyable for you. Therefore, you are more likely to actually get things done. Also, when you are passionate about something you tend to have preexisting knowledge about it. This means that you intimately understand the topic, what makes people excited by it, what common problems are, what people like and want, and what solutions they would be most likely to purchase.

In addition to already having a strong idea about this topic, the problems, and ideal solutions, being passionate about something is enjoyable. Pure and simple. If you have several opportunities outlined, that means you have the opportunity to choose to complete something that you are passionate about. So, if you can actually genuinely enjoy and understand what you are doing, why not?

Step Five: Choose One

With your list narrowed down, it is time to make a choice! The best way to make a choice is actually not to pick what you think will work, but to ask your potential market if they think it will work. There are a few ways that you can test your market out for free, including:

- **Crowdfunding.** Start a crowdfunding campaign and discuss the solution you want to create. Be as detailed as possible and genuinely promote it. If others think it is a good idea, they will help you fund your idea. If they don't, it will simply be overlooked.

If the idea is completely overlooked, you can determine that it is likely not a good one for you to be pursuing.

- **Landing pages.** Creating a landing page is a great way to promote your product and begin the marketing campaign right off of the bat. When you create a landing page, you are essentially asking people to provide you with their email address so that you can inform them of any updates and your upcoming (pending) launch. On the landing page, you can provide a bunch of exciting details about the opportunity and genuinely work toward getting people excited about it with you. If they do, you will recognize this by your email list growing! If it grows rapidly, and you reach a target milestone (e.g., 500-1000 email subscribers), then you know that the idea is a good one and that you should pursue it.

- **Pop-up stores.** Another great way to test the market is to produce a very small amount of the products or provide a very small amount of services and make them available in a pop-up store. This is something you would advertise for and market, as though you were genuinely launching the store. Then, if you make a lot of sales or get a lot of traction, you know that it is a good idea. If you don't, however, you know it may not be a good idea, and you are not out a ton of money from your experiment.

One key factor to consider when you are testing out the market is to pay attention to a timeframe. Set a goal that you want to raise a specific number of funds or emails, or sell a certain number of products or services in a predetermined amount of time. If you do not make it to that point, then you can conclude that it is not likely a strong business idea and that you should choose something else.

Realize that not all opportunities will pan out, no matter how good they look on paper. Furthermore, not everyone will be interested in what you have to offer. Keep looking for new opportunities and testing out new ideas so that in time, you will be confident that you will discover the perfect opportunity for you to pursue.

Clarity

Clarity is not necessarily a step, but rather a by-product of following these steps. However, it is worth mentioning on its own as you do need a strong amount of clarity around your idea if you want it to work out.

When you have clarity, it essentially means that you are very well versed on what you want to create in your business. Think of it this way: a seed is not coded to become a "plant," it is coded to become a "Douglas fir" or a "petunia." Likewise, if your businesses "coding" isn't very specific, you are not going to be able to pursue it as effectively. After all, if you aren't entirely clear on what you are all about, how will you ever explain it to your customers?

If you have an idea and you cannot clearly articulate it, your idea needs clarity. You can get this in two ways: first, by going through the list, you have just been walked through. Go through each of these steps and polish off your idea along the way. You will likely learn a lot about the idea itself, and where it's strengths and weaknesses lie. You will also be able to start developing it. The next area where you will get clarity is when you are actually developing the idea in Chapter 2.

Clarity is absolutely necessary if you are ever going to take a business idea and turn it into a plan, and later a successful business. If you have an idea that you cannot clearly articulate and that you do not fully understand, you will struggle to generate a powerful plan for it. And, if you cannot generate a powerful plan, you will fail at launching a successful business. That is not harsh, it is merely the truth.

After you complete the five steps from this chapter, and through the process of developing your idea in the next chapter, keep the word "clarity" in mind. You will know that you have become clear enough when you can answer the following questions:

- Whom does this product or service serve?
- Why do they want it?
- What is it?
- When would they use it?
- Where is the product or service going to be made available?
- How am I going to provide it?

Answering these questions will ensure that you are equipped with enough clarity to successfully generate a plan and create an entire business off of the idea you have come up with. If you cannot answer all of these questions, you may need to conduct more research. If you still cannot, you may not have a strong enough idea to pursue.

Chapter 2: Developing Your Idea

Developing your idea is the process where you take an opportunity and turn it into a real idea. Here is where you will gain clarity, look for opportunities to expand or improve on your initial idea, and ultimately generate an idea that is strong enough to actually turn into a business plan.

When you are developing an idea, you may find that you have come across an idea that is good but cannot be taken beyond a mere idea. If that happens, do not worry. Instead, go back to Chapter 1 and go through the five-step process to find a new idea. Understand that the development stage is usually where you get to really test your idea to ensure that it is one worth pursuing. Here is how you can develop your idea.

Make a "Plan"

For this test, you do not want to actually pursue a full plan for your idea. Instead, you only want to consider a couple of basic questions. Consider this to be a pretend, or practice plan. If you can effectively answer these questions and they have answers that sound promising, then you may have a good idea on your hands. Here are the questions you need to ask yourself:

- How marketable is this product?

- How long is its lifecycle?

- Is the market big enough?

- What is the five-year projection for it?

- Can I expand on it and come out with different products?

- Is anyone else already doing it? If so, can I reasonably compete?

Although you do not need to answer these questions with completely accurate answers, you do want to get as close to a realistic answer as you can. In doing so, you will discover if the plan you will make later can actually be created in the first place. For example, if you think you have a great idea but later learn that you do not have the ability to remain competitive with the existing market, it may not be a good idea. After all, people will go to where they can get it for cheaper, or better. If you cannot reasonably compete with the existing market, then you may be pursuing a great idea that is already taken.

Consider Your Resources

If you are coming up with an idea that is completely new to you, you may not have any idea as to what your resources are. However, you do want to do some research and take a look. Researching what your potential resources are will give you an idea as to whether or not the plan is viable. If you look into it and learn that it would be too expensive and not profitable enough, you do not want to be getting involved in the market. Instead, you want to look for options that are affordable and that have the potential to earn you the highest amount of profit.

The best way to consider your resources is to consider the funds you already have, the additional funds you would need (and the amount you would pay to acquire them), potential manufacturers you may need, and anything else about the creation and marketing of your product. Pay attention to how much these cost and how you will be paying for them. You want to get a really good idea of how much every single item would cost you, and the amount of money you may make back on it if it sold. If the profit ratio is too low, it may not be worth the risk as you may not be able to get back your money. If you face a strong potential of losing money, it is likely not a good opportunity to be pursuing.

Explore All Options

Take some time and look at all of the different options available to you. Consider the problem you are attempting to solve, and the solution you have come up with. Try and think of any additional solutions that may be available to you, and what other options you may have for solving said problems. Then, look at each one as a viable option. Work through the logistics and potential of each one until you rule out the ones that definitely wouldn't work. Along the way, you should also be able to discover which ones would most likely work, and you may even find "the one."

Along the process of exploring options, also explore how you may be able to slightly adjust or improve the solution you choose. For example, say you decide that you are definitely going to build a tool that businesses can put in their change rooms so clients can take pictures of potential outfits. If you are fixated on this idea, and you have determined that it is a good idea, now you want to push further into that idea. What features can you include that would make this product the most useful? Are there any extra features you can add on that would make this product better? Is there a better design you can use, or any other way that you can improve on the initial idea?

Push the idea you have to its limits. Get as creative as you can, and look at every option available to you. Even look at the potentially strange ones that may seem completely wrong to you from the get-go. The more you exploit the item you are considering creating, the more chances you have of finding the best design that would allow it to fulfill the need effectively.

Answer the Clarity Questions

Once you have developed the idea further, it is time to answer your clarity questions. Although we have already touched down on the basic questions, we are now going to look at them a little deeper. You want to look at them deeper directly about your idea so that you can truly put your idea to the test and decide whether or not it is viable.

In the previous chapter, you tested your idea on the market. Now, you need to test it as an actual potential business. This is where you will find out if this idea would convert into a business plan effectively, or if it would cost you too much money or otherwise become unachievable in the business development process.

- **Who?**

  First, you need to get extremely clear on whom you are serving. What is their demographic? This means you need to determine what gender, age, and location your potential client is in. You should also consider their average income range, how much money they spend on products or services like yours, and where you might be able to find them both online and offline. By being clear on whom you are serving, you can ensure that you have come up with a product that will actually serve that specific demographic. You do not want to attempt to sell something to one demographic that was designed to better appeal to another one. Be very clear on who your demographic is so that everything can be tailored to this person. If you find that your idea is too expensive for their budget, does not serve their demographic effectively, or otherwise has a flaw that causes it not to mold well with this demographic, now is the time to adjust your idea to fit the audience you intend to sell to.

- **What?**

Get very clear on what it is that you are selling your audience. This means that you should not only know about what product or service it is but also about what features it will have. You should also know which of these features will be the most appealing to your audience, as these are the ones you want to ensure are made with the best quality. You will also want to keep these noted so that you can make it very clear in your marketing strategies that these unique features have been made available.

- **When?**

When do you think the person you are selling to would use your product or service? When do they encounter the problem that makes them feel the need to use it in the first place? Get clear about when your audience will use it. This means that you are also very clear on the specific problem it is solving, and when they are most likely to encounter it. For example, for the change room selfie device, your audience would encounter the problem in the change room anytime they are trying on new clothes.

If you are selling a special towel, your audience will encounter the problem when they are getting out of the shower or bath, or maybe they are sweating at the gym. Pay attention to the exact moment they would need your product.

- **Where?**

Where are they going to use it? If applicable, where are they going to store it? When you know where a person will use your product, you can tailor it specifically for that space. For example, if you have invented a special towel just for the gym, your client may not want something that is bulky and will take up a lot of space in their bag. Therefore, creating a product that is easy to roll up and store in a small amount of space makes it easier for them to keep it with them. Since they are storing it in their bag, and it will be sweaty at some point, you may also consider creating some form of special carrying feature that allows them to keep the sweat contained and not soaking into other objects in their bag. If you are selling a service, consider where they will use it. For example, a self-help course. Where are they going to be when they are using your course? How can you enhance the course to make it extremely user-friendly in this environment? Paying attention to these key features means that you can add a convenience element, which is something that everyone looks for. They want to know that when they will use the product, it is appropriate for the place they are using it in. The more convenient it is to use it in that location, the better.

- **Why?**

Why does your audience want your product in the first place? Why would they buy yours and not someone else's? You want to consider what is special about your product. What helps it stand apart from other products that are available? As well, do they really need it? If so, why is it so important? If you can clearly define why someone would want your product now, while you are still in the idea stages, you make it much easier for you to generate something that someone would actually want. Remember, the first question they will ask and answer to themselves about your product or service will be "why?" If they can come up with a great answer really quickly (or you provide them with one), they will be much more likely to go ahead and purchase your product. If they cannot determine why it would be important or worth the investment, they likely won't spend anything on it. As well, you need to outline why your product is so much better. Is it more affordable? Does it have better features? Is it higher quality? What makes your product distinctive from someone else's, enough so that they would want to purchase from you and not your competitor?

- **How?**

  How is your product going to enhance the life of your client? How have you made it so that this is something they cannot live without? What features have you added that makes it so special? Being able to effectively understand how your product is enhancing someone's life means that you can easily let them know as well, meaning it will make it far easier for you to market the product.

The ultimate way to determine if you are clear enough or not is to complete the following statement:

"My product is a _____, which enhances my client's life by _____. It will be used by _____, and purchased by _____. They will be willing to pay up to $___.___ for this product, as long as it does _____ for them. They will want it most when they are _____, as this is when they face the problem of _____. I have a competitive edge because _____, meaning people will want to purchase from me."

Here is an example of a completed copy of this statement, so you can see what yours should look like:

"My product is a selfie device to use in change rooms, which enhances my client's life by reminding them which clothes they looked great in, and which they didn't like as much. It will be used by women between the ages of 20-50 who like to shop around for the best deals and find the best clothes, and it will be purchased by fashion stores. They will be willing to pay up to $19.99 for this product, as long as it does the job of helping their clients pick the best clothes for them. They will want it most when they are helping their clients decide which clothes they should choose, as this is when they face the problem of trying to recall which clothes they liked the most. I have a competitive edge because no one else is doing this, meaning people will want to purchase from me."

If your idea does not pass the clarity test, meaning that you are not clear enough to answer any of the above questions, you will need to either take more time and further research the idea or pick a new one. Before anything is moved into a true planning stage, you should always be certain that you have become completely clear about these answers. If you are not, you will not have enough information to plan your business properly, and therefore it will not work out properly.

If you have answered all of the questions effectively, you are ready for the idea-to-plan conversion stage! First off, congratulations on coming up with an awesome plan! And second, good luck in taking it to the next level!

Chapter 3: Building Your Plans

Now that you have a great idea, it is time to turn it into a plan! If your idea has successfully passed the clarity test, you know it is ready to be turned into a reality. So, you can begin the conversion process! In this chapter, you will learn the basics of turning your idea into a plan. Before you create the blueprint itself, however, you have to do some dreaming! In this chapter, we will dream of a (realistic) future for your plan. This will give you something to look forward to and focus on when it comes to building the actual blueprint for you to follow step-by-step. If you are ready, let's get dreaming!

What Do You Want from This Plan?

First, you need to consider what you want from this plan. What are you going in with the intention of getting out of it? Do you want lots of sales? Are you hoping to build a recognizable brand name? Is this an opportunity for you to dip your toes in the business world? What is your unique reasoning for creating this plan?

When you are considering what you want from your plan, you can consider yourself and your customers. Consider what has compelled you to create the plan in the first place, and what sparked the idea in your mind. When you can get a clear idea of the roots, it becomes easier to get an idea of what your goal is as well. You want to look on both ends of the spectrum. Knowing what sparked the idea and what you want as the end result is the best way to establish some goals and create a plan that will get you from start to finish. Spend a few minutes pondering this so that you are extremely clear on where you want to go.

When you look at where you want to go, look from a personal perspective and look from a business perspective. This will ensure that your goal will fit your needs, but also that it will work together with your business. For example, perhaps your unique purpose is to pursue this so that you can generate a residual income stream. However, from your businesses perspective, you are pursuing this so that you can fulfill a need that you have discovered while attempting to recall which clothes you liked the most after a long day of shopping. As you can see, your personal reason is about you, and your business reason is about fulfilling a need for your customer. This is what your two reasons for why you are pursuing what you are pursuing, and what has made you want to do it in the first place.

What Do You Think Is Realistic? Why?

When you are creating a plan, it always needs to be realistic. Of course, in the dreaming stages, you can go as big as you want. However, it is typically also a good idea to create a dream that is realistic. This way you can ensure that your plan is one that you can actually fulfill, and not one that will be too hard to attain. Many people are told to "dream as big as you can," and this is valuable in many respects. However, when it comes to designing a business plan, it can actually take away from your successful ability to do so. While you certainly want to dream large, you never want to dream unrealistically large. Instead, dream big and then work as hard as you can to reach that dream. If you do, dream bigger!

Consider Product Creation

Take some time to consider what you would want the product creation process to look like. When it comes to getting products created, you should think about how you want it done. Are you using a manufacturer? Are you using a wholesaler? Are you creating it yourself? How are the products going to be packaged? Is this a generic packaging idea, or does it somehow contribute to the product or the user experience? Create a basic plan for how you want this process to look. Consider how many units you would need, what would be essential for the process to work in accordance with your idea, and any other elements that you may think of in the process. At this point you are only brainstorming, so you don't necessarily need to go deep into your specific ideas. You simply need to have an idea of what you are looking for in the first place.

If you are creating a service, there are still many things you can consider when it comes to the creation process. For example, what platform do you want to use to host this service on? What elements are you going to invest in that will make the service complete? How are you going to deliver the service? Is there anything you can do to enhance the delivery process and make it more enjoyable for your audience? Consider every aspect of the service creation and any products or services that you would need to create and deliver the service to your audience.

Consider Marketing

What would your idea marketing look like when it comes to marketing your product or service? Do you plan on using the online space primarily, or the offline space? Or, are you going to use a bit of both? Once you have decided where you want your marketing to take place, start brainstorming marketing strategies you can use to get your product or service in front of your audience. Look for every opportunity you have to get it out there so that you have a clear idea of what is available to you. At this point, because you are only brainstorming, do not consider what different marketing strategies would cost you. Instead, simply push your ideas as far as you can to look for several methods of marketing that may be available for you. For example, your online marketing list could look like this:

- Banner Ads

- Social media ads

- Pay-per-click ads

- Sponsored blog posts

- Influencers

- Word of mouth

- Networking

- Strategically placed videos

- Blog posts

- Referral program

Consider as many different opportunities that may be available for you. Even go as big as considering billboards, blimps, and other major marketing strategies if you are looking at offline marketing strategies. Remember, just because you might not be able to reasonably afford any of these marketing strategies doesn't mean you cannot think about them. The idea behind thinking as big and creative as you possibly can is that you may discover unique marketing opportunities that other companies aren't already using. This is how new trends are born every day, so don't be afraid to go out on a limb and see what is available to you! Just because it is unconventional doesn't mean it can't work for you!

Consider Sales

You want to think about the selling process of your products, also. Brainstorm what selling will be like for you. Are you going to funnel your audience to a website and have them purchase through a link? Or are you going to have them communicate with a sales employee (or you directly) so that they can discover if the product is right for them to begin with? How are the sales going to be conducted? There are many different opportunities when it comes to selling both products and services. Having your own website and selling directly through there is a popular way, but you can also sell through host websites such as Amazon or Shopify. There are also offline sales which can be done in many ways. For example, you might sell your items at someone else's store, open your own store, or consider a store-free way of sales such as network marketing.

Once again, look at every option that is available to you. While you are at it, consider how each option would work.

Some options are completely unrealistic for certain products or services, so it is important that you really emphasize on the ones that are most likely to be feasible for your sales process. While you are at it, look to see if there are any customizations or adjustments that you can make so that the sales process is even better.

Consider the Customer Experience

The customer experience is absolutely everything when it comes to business. Knowing what your business will look like from a customer's perspective means that you can completely design a business that will appeal to your customers. Not only will your business sell incredible products, but you will also be given the opportunity to customize the experience so that when customers think about it, they think about you. Think of companies like Apple, for example. Apple does not just sell products, they sell experiences. When you visit an Apple store, you are greeted by their customer service team. One of the members often helps you with your sales process, and they tend to use Apple products to conduct the experience. You can even pay directly through their company iPhones with your representative without ever having to wait in line for help. There are tables everywhere allowing you to sit and try the products, and they even run in-store help classes to teach you to use them. Your sales rep will even help you set up your new device and ensure that it is working and you understand how to use it. Even beyond the customer service experience, the process of opening the box is an experience as well. Everything, even right down to the stickers protecting the surfaces of your new device, is completely designed with the intention of you having a phenomenal experience. It is highly likely that this entire experience is why so many of Apple's customers are fiercely loyal to their company.

When you are designing your own business, you have the opportunity to look at the customer's experience from this perspective as well. You have the power to choose whether or not you want to design an experience so incredible that your customers are eager to come back and experience it again. While having such an in-depth experience is not necessary, and maybe not even realistic for many new companies, it is certainly worth considering what you can do to make your customer experience more memorable.

How can you design an experience that is convenient, effective, enjoyable, and memorable? What are the different ways that you can make it so that your customer is genuinely excited to invest money in your products and services and to experience your company for themselves? Even though this may seem over the top, customizing a user experience for your audience is a great way to make them want to choose your company over anyone else's. Many people purchase from a place of emotion versus from a place of logic. If you can appeal to your audience's emotions by making the process positive, exciting, and enjoyable, they will be far more likely to share it with their own network and get them excited about coming to experience your company. Consider this part of the equation as much as you can and brainstorm all of the options you have to enhance your customer's experience so that they want to choose you over any other company.

Consider Your Back End Experience

There are two sides of businesses: the part the customer sees, and the part they don't see. Even though your customer does not see or even directly experience the backend part of the business, it is still important for you to consider this part. This is the part that directly affects both you and the customer. For the customer, a faulty back-end system will result in the entire customer experience falling apart, no matter how much you invest in it. Therefore, having your backend running as good as your front end, if not better, is the best way to ensure your customer experience is protected.

For you, the back end experience reflects how you will experience your business. The biggest thing you need to consider here is: how much do you want to be involved in this business? If you want to be heavily involved, you can take on many more responsibilities and tasks and be involved in as many ways as you comfortably can. If, however, you do not want to be overly involved, you can start looking at options to help you step back and allow others to run your business for you. Say, for example, you do not want to be involved at all. You could consider hiring a marketing team and then running an online drop shipping business. Between your marketing team and your drop shipping suppliers, you would have enough people on board that you would not need to be overly involved in the process. If you want to be more involved but not heavily involved, you can start selecting the tasks that you want to be involved in and then look for ways to delegate the rest to other people.

Remember when you are brainstorming this part that you are likely going to have to have a large amount of involvement in the beginning stages. Because you are the one building the business, it will be necessary for you to have all-hands-on-deck until you are in a place where you can comfortably pass the tasks along to someone else. Some businesses will have a shorter involved-to-uninvolved time. For example, a successful drop shipping company truly only requires you to hire a marketing team. As long as you can generate some sales quickly, it will be effortless for you to hire a marketing team and put them in your position so that you can step back. If, however, you want to start an entire store-front company, you will have to be involved for longer. Not only will you have to be present to ensure that your company is built and grows the way you want it to, but you will also have to be present to train your employees, at least at first. Once you have gotten this far, however, you can then step back as much as you want to.

Honestly consider the amount of involvement you are willing to commit to your company. It is crucial that you realize that you will have to be involved at first, no matter what. If you are not interested in being involved, it may be a good idea to consider an alternative business idea that you can turn into a plan. That is because if you are not interested in being involved, there is a good chance that you will not be able to turn your business into a success on any level. Make sure you are genuinely interested in being involved at first so that you have the power to turn your business into a success.

Chapter 4: A Blueprint for Success

Now that you have brainstormed your idea and generated a basic plan for what you want from your business, it is time to build a real business plan that will get you there! In this chapter, we will explore the most important steps required for you to get your business idea and dream into a workable blueprint that you can follow so that you can generate success. I hope you are ready to bring your dreams to a reality now!

Executive Summary

You want to use this space in your plan to briefly tell the person reading your plan what your company is all about! This is where you get to share your idea and explain how you plan to make it a success. In this space, you can generate a mission statement, explain the product or service you are creating, and any basic information you may have to share about the employee and leadership structure for your business, as well as where it will be located. You can also share information about your finances and what your growth plans are if you intend on asking anyone for funding using this plan.

Company Description

You want to give your reader a detailed insight as to what your company is all about. Here, you want to explain what the problem is that you intend to solve, and how you solve this problem with your products or services. You want to be very specific in this section. List out the exact demographic you plan to serve, and what competitive advantages you have when it comes to serving them. Identify every advantage you have and explain why this will help you turn your business into a success.

Market Analysis

Hopefully, when you were coming up with your idea, you did some basic market research. This would have been done in the form of hosting a landing page, a crowdsourcing campaign, or any other form of marketing that would enable potentially interested buyers to show their interest in your unique company, product, or service.

In addition to that, you also want to look into market specifics. How large is your market? How much money are they spending, and is this number growing or shrinking? How well are other businesses in your industry doing? Is their growth increasing drastically, at a plateau, or declining? Look for any trends and themes you may be able to find that help you identify how well the market is, and how you can position yourself in the market so that you can reach your target audience. Be very thorough and detailed in this section.

Organization and Management

Be sure to tell your reader exactly how you plan on structuring the management and leadership in your company. Are you a sole proprietor? If so, do you have anyone helping you? If you intend on running a corporation, who are you going to hire to run your business for you? How is the management structure going to be designed? Will there be many managers, a tier of managers, or a single manager?

You also want to describe the legal organization and structure of your business. Are you going to remain a sole proprietor, or do you intend to incorporate your business? If so, what form of corporation structure or partnership structure do you intend to use? Create an organizational chart that will help you graph out exactly how your company will be run, based on who is in charge and where they sit on the tier.

Service or Product Line

Here, you want to get really detailed about the products and services you are offering. You want to take some time to explain how these will benefit your customer, and why they would be interested in buying it. You also want to consider the lifespan of your product. This means, how long are people going to use it, and how long are they going to be interested in buying it?

In addition to explaining your product, you want to explain more about the legal side of your product as well. What plans do you have for intellectual property? Are you going to (or in the process of) filing for copyright or a patent? If you are still in the process of researching, be honest about this and explain why. You also want to explain what research you are doing and what needs to be done so that your reader knows exactly where you are, what you are looking at, and where you are going with product development.

Marketing and Sales

There are infinite types of marketing strategies, so there is no true blueprint you can use when it comes to designing your marketing strategy. Instead, you need to take the brainstorm you made in the previous chapter and choose the strategies that will work best for your company, your product, and your budget. Explain what your marketing and sales strategy looks like based on this information.

In addition to creating a new strategy for the immediate future, you also need to design a growth strategy. This should go into detail about how you will evolve your strategy and what changes will be made as you hit different milestones. Ultimately, you want to focus on using this section to help you explain how you will attract customers, as well as retain them.

You also want to use this part of the process to explain how the sale will actually work. Remember in the previous chapter how you got to brainstorm the sales process? Now you get to choose which strategy you want to use and describe how it will look for your customers. Make sure you explain this part, as you will be using this as a reference for when it comes to designing the financial part of your blueprint.

Be very thorough and clear on this part of your business blueprint as this is the area that will set the tone for everything else. If you have a strong plan here, you will be able to have strong financial forecasts for the future. If you do not, then no matter how strong your forecasts are, your strategies will not be strong enough to turn them into a reality.

Revenue Streams

It is important to know where the money is coming from in your business! When you are designing your blueprint, explain all of the different ways your business plans on bringing in an income. Be sure to talk about revenue directly from sales, but look at other routes as well. Is there anything you have to offer as an add-on? Are you doing anything else to generate revenue? Describe every income-producing aspect of your business with detail.

You should also explain if you have the intention of building new revenue streams in the future. For example, if you are building a new and revolutionary e-reader to sell, naturally you will generate revenue from the sales of the product. You may also plan that in the future you will have a fully independently-owned library as well, similar to a Kindle. In that case, your library would be an additional source of revenue. If you plan on hiring writers to write exclusive books for your e-reader, that would be another source of revenue. Outline all existing and intended revenue sources that you have for your business, and explain when future ones will come into play, if there are any.

Funding Request

If you are requesting funds to assist you with launching or running your business, this will be the part of your blueprint or business plan where you get to make your request. Here, you want to be very clear and specific. State exactly what you are asking for, how you intend to use and manage the funds, and what the result will be from that usage.

Typically, if you are asking for funding, you want to ask for enough to help you over a five-year period. With that in mind, create a five-year plan for how much you would ask for, how you would use it, and how this will benefit the growth of your business.

You should also use this part to explain what method you would like to use to acquire the funding. For example, are you asking for a loan, or do you intend to sell a part of your company in return for the finances? In either scenario, be very specific. If it is a loan, for example, explain how much you intend to borrow, how soon you will pay it back, and any terms you would like applied to the loan. If you are asking to sell a portion of the company, explain how much they are getting and any terms of that sale.

Financial Projections

In addition to a funding request, if you are making one, you need to share your financial projections. If you do not have a funding request, you should still share your projections anyway. This is where you get to convince your reader that you will be able to generate financial success in your business, and what type of success you are expecting.

Remember, you want to use your marketing and sales strategies here to support your projections. If you are making exceptionally high projections but have a weak strategy, you are not going to be able to support your claim adequately and the reader will likely not believe you. However, if you have a strong system supporting a strong claim, you are more likely to be able to convince your reader that you are being realistic about these claims.

If you remember from your optional funding request, you wanted to make a 5-year projection of the funds you would need and how you would use these funds to grow your business. You want to ensure that you also make your financial projections on a 5-year projection as well. If you have a funding request, you should make this as an extension of the request. For that reason, it should accurately reflect the request you have made. If you do not, this can be a stand-alone projection.

Appendix

Your appendix is where you get to share al supporting documents and materials related to your business plan or blueprint. Any research you have conducted or cited from should be included here, as well as any official documents, such as copyrights or patents. Credit histories, resumes, pictures of your products, licenses, permits, letters of reference, and anything else that you have which may support your business can also be included in this section.

After you have created your business plan, you ultimately have a blueprint for you to follow! This plan will give you very specific instructions, which you have laid out, to help you move forward. As long as you conduct your research properly in this section, you should have plenty of information that will help you in moving forward, thus giving you a clear action plan to take your earliest steps!

Chapter 5: Don't Forget These Important Tips!

Naturally, you are still going to have some questions when it comes to moving forward with your business. After all, your business plan is a great in-depth resource to help you move forward, but it may not cover absolutely everything that you are curious about! For that reason, we have included an extra chapter filled with steps from successful entrepreneurs who have managed to turn their great ideas into businesses. Using these tips, your idea, your passion, and your blueprint, you can begin running a wildly successful business! Recognize that due to the nature of the business, some of these tips may not apply to you. For example, if one is intended for online businesses and you run a brick-and-mortar store, there is a good chance the tip will not work well for you. However, it is strongly encouraged that you read them anyway, as you never know where inspiration will come from.

No Matter What, Make a Business Plan

Many people are unaware of the impact a business plan actually has when it comes to running a business. If you have never run one before, you may believe that a business plan is only created for you to approach potential funding sources to help you when it comes to launching your business. While this certainly is a powerful benefit, it is not the only benefit you reap from having a business plan.

In fact, developing a business plan is more like creating your own custom blueprint. This is where you get to brainstorm your idea and convert it into an actionable plan. The business plan itself not only gives you an idea of where you are going, but it also gives you something to measure your success by. Since your business plan is an official document, you can use this plan to look back on at any point in the future to see how well you are doing against your projections. If you notice that you are underperforming, you may want to adjust your projections to be more realistic. You can also review your marketing and sales strategies and see if there is anything you can do to increase your success in the business. Alternatively, you may find that you are performing much better than intended. If this is the case, you will want to revise your projections to reflect your growth. You may also want to adjust your action plan to ensure that you can accommodate the growth. If you find that you are underperforming or overperforming, don't worry too much at first. It is difficult to project exactly how a company will perform if you have no existing experience with that specific company. Once you start getting some real numbers, however, you can adjust your projections to reflect these real numbers. Then, you can adjust your plan.

Make a Business Map

Your business plan is a great blueprint to use to help you make a business map, too. A business map is exactly what it sounds like: a map of what specific action you will take to get to where you want to go. For example, if you have determined that you project to make $100,000 in sales in five years using your strategy, now you can create a business map for exactly how you will get there. In other words, how are you going to implement your strategy? If you intend to get your business live online, what can you do to make it go live? Map out everything from hiring a web designer to designing your website and marketing it on your map.

Essentially, you want to create a business map that will include all of your major goals. This will be your "master map" that you can refer to any time you are curious about which major goal you are working toward. This will give you an overall sense of direction. Then, you can also use this map to create mini-maps or task sheets. For example, maybe your map says to hire a web designer so you can get a website live in a set amount of time. If that is the case, you now know that you need to create a task list that includes you interviewing designers and hiring one, then going through the building process. You can set aside time to come up with an idea of what you want your website to look like, and any other requirements that come along with launching your business. Then, when you are ready, you can execute all of the tasks and reach your milestones as per your business map's layout.

Having a business map gives you a sense of direction and ensures that you are regularly working toward your major goals. With your map, you want to make sure you are being specific, but not too specific. Focus on major goals like "get website live," "launch marketing campaign," "get first 100 customers", "make first $10,000 in sales", "launch new product," and so forth until you land at your ultimate goal, which is your five-year projected position. Let the specific parts of each goal come in later when you are actually executing them.

Set Aside $200

One big tip that many entrepreneurs recommend is that you set aside just $200 at first. That may sound small, but that small amount can save you a major amount in the long run.

Ultimately, you want to use this $200 to invest in a "test". This is the money you will invest in designing a landing page and building an email list, or marketing a crowdfunding campaign. You want to use this money to launch your idea, not your business. Then, if you get great responses, you know that you can use more money or request funding to help you actually launch the business. You can use the data you have collected from this experiment to help you create realistic projections, also. However, if you do not get a good turn out from your test, you know that the idea is likely not a good one to pursue and that you should not invest any more money in it. This way, you only lost $200, rather than losing several hundred or thousands of dollars getting started, only to later find out that your projections were false.

Start Small

There is a saying by people in the entrepreneurial world that says "start with bullets, not cannons." This means that you want to be modest when you start your business. Many people want to run out of the gates hot, and dream of how they will approach major corporations and get their products sold everywhere. While this is a noble dream, it is not a realistic one. This is why, back in the brainstorming stage, we mentioned that you should have two dreams: your overall dream, and a realistic dream for right now.

Essentially, you want to start by following the realistic dream. Look for opportunities to invest small, test the idea in the real world, and collect more information. If you pass the $200 test, then go on to invest one or two thousand. If you pass that test, invest a little more. Investing in smaller increments and then gradually investing more based on your results is the best way to ensure that you never invest more than a product or service will earn you in return. In the end, it saves you from losing money by going too big right off of the bat.

Start with 10 Customers

Following the idea of starting small, many entrepreneurs say start with just 10 customers. In other words, invest enough in your business that you can attract and fulfill the sale for 10 customers. Once you have, you can gradually increase your sales numbers until you reach your desired projections. Starting with only 10 customers is a great way to help you start modest but reasonable. 10 customers are not hard to find, especially if you have a good product or service on hand. However, if you find that getting just 10 customers is too hard, there is a good chance that this is because the product or service is not attractive enough.

An important note to remember is that if you genuinely tried and could not get 10 customers, it is best not to assume that it is because you do not know how to market. Instead, assume it is because you do not have a strong enough idea that will make sales. Many people want to blame themselves and insist that their idea is strong enough to make sales, despite their sales track record showing otherwise. Even if you are not necessarily great at sales or marketing, a good product or service will still manage to attract at least a handful of people. If you cannot, then do not pursue the idea.

Critique the Idea

Get honest criticism about the idea that you have. Many people are eager to say "yeah, great idea!" because they don't want to hurt our feelings. A good way to refine your idea is to ask people to give you honest criticism, assuring them that they are not going to hurt your feelings. If you cannot get this from people you know, try making a questionnaire online and asking a handful of people to fill it out. Getting true criticism is a good way to test where the faults lie early on, rather than assuming that you have worked it all out and everything is good to go. Your actual marketing audience is the best place to test, so look to find ways to request criticism from them directly. This will ensure that you get their perspective and can refine your idea before going full-scale with it.

Conclusion

Congratulations for reading *"How to Create a Business:* The Best Way to Plan and Develop Your Big Idea"!

I hope this book was successful in helping you find a great idea if you didn't already have one, and develop it to the point that you can create your own business blueprint from it! With the chapters in this book, you were guided through the process of picking a great idea, developing it enough to ensure that it is valid, and then using brainstorming and planning techniques to transform it into a real business plan!

The next step is to take your time and ensure that you fully research your marketability and that your business is fail-proof. While you cannot absolutely guarantee it is fail-proof of course, being very critical of it early on and developing it carefully is the best way to ensure that your business will be a success. Remember, invest small, but stay dedicated. As you generate success, invest more. You never want to invest more than an idea is truly worth, so refrain from making this mistake by taking your time and putting one foot in front of the other, rather than leaping toward the end goal. Creating a proper business map can help you with this process!

Lastly, if you enjoyed this book, I ask that you, please take the time to rate it on Amazon Kindle. Your honest feedback would be greatly appreciated!

Thank you!

Book Description

Are you ready to design a business that is the next big hit? Maybe you want something that is timeless, like hair ties, or something that is trendy and hits big, like fidget spinners. Or, maybe you don't entirely care what "it" is, as long as it helps you generate a massive income!

If you have an idea, or if you don't, this book was designed just for you. "How to Create a Business: The Best Way to Plan and Develop Your Big Idea" will walk you through the process of finding an idea if you don't have one, and developing your idea if you do. You will be walked through thorough steps to help you test your idea and ensure that it has the potential to be the next big deal.

Once you have tested your idea, you will be walked through the process of turning it into a true business plan, and later using that business plan to generate your actionable idea! You will also be given tips by successful entrepreneurs to help you ensure that you approach your business in the best way possible. This will be especially helpful in assisting you to determine how much time and money you should invest at each stage to avoid losing any capital!

If you are ready to be walked through the process in a step-by-step fashion, then you have found the perfect book for you. Come on, let's turn your dreams into a reality and help your business become the next big thing! Are you ready?

www.ingramcontent.com/pod-product-compliance
Lightning Source LLC
Chambersburg PA
CBHW071233220526
45468CB00002B/830